core belief

Bible Study Series
for senior high

WHY Suffering MATTERS

Group

Loveland, Colorado

Why Suffering Matters
Core Belief Bible Study Series
Copyright © 1997 Group Publishing, Inc.

Credits
Editors: Lisa Baba Lauffer and Joani Schultz
Managing Editor: Michael D. Warden
Chief Creative Officer: Joani Schultz
Copy Editor: Julie Meiklejohn
Art Director: Lisa Chandler
Cover Art Director: Helen H. Lannis
Cover Designer/Assistant Art Director: Bill Fisher
Computer Graphic Artist: Kari K. Monson
Photographer: Craig DeMartino
Production Manager: Gingar Kunkel

Unless otherwise noted, Scriptures quoted from The Youth Bible, New Century Version, copyright © 1991 by Word Publishing, Dallas, Texas 75039. Used by permission.

ISBN 0-7644-0879-8

10 9 8 7 6 5 4 3 2   06 05 04 03 02 01 00 99 98 97

Printed in the United States of America.

core belief

Bible Study Series
for senior high

contents:

the Core Belief: ▼Suffering

We live in a society that shuns pain. We avoid anything that causes us discomfort, and when we suffer, we wonder what we've done wrong.

Sometimes the answer is "nothing."

Try as we might, we can't stave off the entrance of suffering into our lives. It's a part of our world. From the instant that Adam and Eve took that bite of forbidden fruit, humanity was doomed to suffer. This wasn't part of God's original plan—he had created a perfect world with no sorrow or loss. But with sin came pain and death.

We don't understand it. We try to reconcile the idea of a loving God with the disaster we see in our world and experience in our own lives. But when we stop resisting it, when we respond to it with faith in God, God can use suffering to teach us some of the most valuable lessons we can learn.

the ▼Helpful Stuff

the ▼Studies

▼Suffering as a Core Christian Belief

- Why does God let people starve to death?
- Why do bad things happen to good people?
- How could a loving God let innocent children suffer and die?

It's easy for teenagers to see the suffering around them and question how God could let such things happen.

We don't have all the answers to the problem of suffering, but kids need to be able to work through the questions and discover the answers that the Bible does give. Only then will they be able to affirm their faith in our loving and all-powerful God.

This study course will help your kids understand the reasons for and the purposes of suffering in their lives. First, they'll focus on ways they experience **emotional pain** when something hinders their dreams from becoming reality. As they consider the purpose of their pain, they'll discover that God can use suffering to enable them to trust him more and more every day.

In the second study, kids will explore the meaning of **commitment,** especially the costs of dedicating themselves to something or someone. They'll evaluate times they've suffered for a cause they believed in. Then they'll examine the truth that while a relationship with Christ comes at a cost, it's the most worthy cause for which they could ever suffer.

But this study course won't leave kids feeling doomed to suffer alone. Instead, kids will explore the truth that God is with them whenever they experience suffering. No matter how alone they feel, God always accompanies them through the obstacles they face on life's journey. They'll discover this truth as they address their personal experiences with **broken homes.**

Finally, your students will evaluate their level of **busyness** and examine whether they constantly occupy their time because of an ulterior motive: to avoid facing their suffering. As they evaluate their level of pain avoidance, they'll realize that God not only stands with them when they hurt, but he also gives them everything they need to cope with their suffering.

*For a more comprehensive look at this Core Christian Belief, read Group's **Get Real: Making Core Christian Beliefs Relevant to Teenagers.***

DEPTHFINDER

HOW THE BIBLE DESCRIBES SUFFERING

To help you effectively guide your kids toward this Core Christian Belief, use these overviews as a launching point for a more in-depth study of suffering.

● **Suffering is an intrusion into God's creation.** God created a world free of any pain or suffering. When Adam and Eve sinned, sickness, pain, suffering, and death corrupted creation. Through Jesus' suffering and death on the cross, sin, suffering, and death will ultimately be defeated. When Jesus returns and establishes the new heaven and new earth, Christians will live with him, free from pain and sorrow. But until then, because humanity has chosen a path of sin, God allows suffering as a consequence of that sin (Genesis 1:31; 3:15-19; Job 2:6-7; Isaiah 65:17-20; Romans 8:19-22; and Revelation 21:1-8).

● **Suffering is a mystery for humans.** It's difficult for us to understand how God can be loving and all-powerful but allow faithful followers or innocent children to suffer. So we have three choices: reject the idea that God is loving; reject the idea that God is all-powerful; or accept by faith that our loving, all-powerful God allows suffering for good reasons. Sometimes faith requires us to accept what we can't understand because we trust the One who is in control (Job 1–3; Psalms 37:7-24; 73:1-20; Romans 8:18-19; and 2 Corinthians 4:16-18; 12:7-10).

● **We suffer because we live in a sin-cursed world.** In general, suffering is a consequence of the sin in our world. For example, the suffering of a group of people—such as a community or nation—can be the result of the people's sin. Sometimes individuals suffer because of their leaders' or their parents' sins. And sometimes individual suffering results from the individual's sin. God may also allow suffering to discipline people, much as a human parent might discipline a child to correct wrong behavior (Numbers 14:31-33; Psalm 119:67; Jeremiah 13:21-27; Luke 13:1-5; Acts 5:1-11; 1 Corinthians 11:29-30; and Galatians 6:7-8).

● **Suffering is a part of human redemption.** Jesus had to suffer to make eternal life and peace with God possible for us. To defeat sin and suffering for our sake, Jesus had to endure tremendous suffering and rejection, even though he had never sinned. He suffered in our place so that we might one day be free from all suffering (Luke 9:22; 24:46; Acts 17:3; 26:22-23; Hebrews 2:10-15; 9:24-28; and 1 Peter 3:18).

● **Suffering can be a means of spiritual growth.** Like Jesus, Christians are also called to suffer in this life. But God promises to be with us through it all. To God, our faith and obedience are more important than our comfort. And sometimes suffering is necessary to produce a more faithful, enduring follower (Psalm 66:8-12; Matthew 28:20; Romans 5:3-5; 8:28, 34-39; 2 Corinthians 12:7-10; James 1:2-4, 12; and 1 Peter 1:6-9).

● **Suffering can allow us to participate in Jesus' suffering.** Faithful Christians who suffer for their faith should view that suffering as a privilege. We share in Jesus' suffering when we are persecuted because of our faith in him. Our suffering doesn't make us more righteous, but through it we can demonstrate and strengthen our faith in Jesus by enduring our suffering with joy. And we can be confident that God doesn't allow suffering without also providing the strength to stand up under it (Matthew 16:24-25; Acts 5:41-42; 20:22-24; Romans 8:17; Philippians 1:27-30; 3:10; and 1 Peter 4:1-2, 13-14).

● **God wants us to respond to suffering with faith.** Christians, like everyone else, will experience suffering in this life. But as followers of God, we're to respond to suffering by striving to draw closer to God. For example, when we suffer we should ask God for wisdom or insight into the cause. And we should confess any known sin. And any time we suffer, we can cry out to God for strength or relief (Psalms 10; 13; 35; 51:1-12; 142; and James 1:5).

Whether we like it or not, suffering is a reality of life. If your kids don't experience it much themselves, they certainly see it around them. And it's an issue that could cause them to reject God if it makes them see him as less than loving. So help your kids deal with this important issue as they learn what the Bible says about God and suffering.

CORE CHRISTIAN BELIEF OVERVIEW

Here are the twenty-four Core Christian Belief categories that form the backbone of Core Belief Bible Study Series:

The Nature of God	Jesus Christ	The Holy Spirit
Humanity	Evil	Suffering
Creation	The Spiritual Realm	The Bible
Salvation	Spiritual Growth	Personal Character
God's Justice	Sin & Forgiveness	The Last Days
Love	The Church	Worship
Authority	Prayer	Family
Service	Relationships	Sharing Faith

Look for Group's Core Belief Bible Study Series books in these other Core Christian Beliefs!

about

Bible Study Series
for senior high

Think for a moment about your young people. When your students walk out of your youth program after they graduate from junior high or high school, what do you want them to know? What foundation do you want them to have so they can make wise choices?

You probably want them to know the essentials of the Christian faith. You want them to base everything they do on the foundational truths of Christianity. Are you meeting this goal?

If you have any doubt that your kids will walk into adulthood knowing and living by the tenets of the Christian faith, then you've picked up the right book. All the books in Group's Core Belief Bible Study Series encourage young people to discover the essentials of Christianity and to put those essentials into practice. Let us explain...

What Is Group's Core Belief Bible Study Series?

Group's Core Belief Bible Study Series is a biblically in-depth study series for junior high and senior high teenagers. This Bible study series utilizes four defining commitments to create each study. These "plumb lines" provide structure and continuity for every activity, study, project, and discussion. They are:

● **A Commitment to Biblical Depth**—Core Belief Bible Study Series is founded on the belief that kids not only *can* understand the deeper truths of the Bible but also *want* to understand them. Therefore, the activities and studies in this series strive to explain the "why" behind every truth we explore. That way, kids learn principles, not just rules.

● **A Commitment to Relevance**—Most kids aren't interested in abstract theories or doctrines about the universe. They want to know how to live successfully right now, today, in the heat of problems they can't ignore. Because of this, each study connects a real-life need with biblical principles that speak directly to that need. This study series finally bridges the gap between Bible truths and the real-world issues kids face.

● **A Commitment to Variety**—Today's young people have been raised in a sound bite world. They demand variety. For that reason, no two meetings in this study series are shaped exactly the same.

● **A Commitment to Active and Interactive Learning**—Active learning is learning by doing. Interactive learning simply takes active learning a step further by having kids teach each other what they've learned. It's a process that helps kids internalize and remember their discoveries.

For a more detailed description of these concepts, see the section titled "Why Active and Interactive Learning Works With Teenagers" beginning on page 57.

So how can you accomplish all this in a set of four easy-to-lead Bible studies? By weaving together various "power" elements to produce a fun experience that leaves kids challenged and encouraged.

Turn the page to take a look at some of the power elements used in this series.

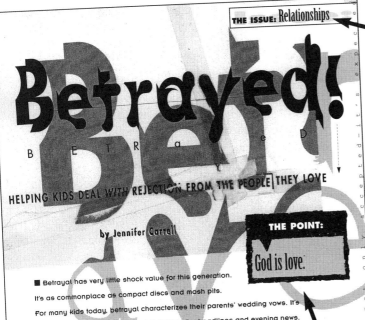

THE ISSUE: Relationships

Betrayed!

HELPING KIDS DEAL WITH REJECTION FROM THE PEOPLE THEY LOVE

by Jennifer Garrell

THE POINT:

God is love.

■ Betrayal has very little shock value for this generation. It's as commonplace as compact discs and mosh pits. For many kids today, betrayal characterizes their parents' wedding vows. It's part of their curriculum at school; it defines the headlines and evening news. Betrayal is not only accepted—it's expected. ■ At the heart of such acceptance lies the belief that nothing is absolute. No vow, no law, no promise can be trusted. Relationships are betrayed at the earliest convenience. Repeatedly, kids see that something called "love" lasts just as long as it's ... ... permanence. But deep inside, they hunger to see a ...

The Study
AT A GLANCE

SECTION	MINUTES	WHAT STUDENTS WILL DO	SUPPLIES
Discussion Starter	up to 5	JUMP-START—Identify some of the most common themes in today's movies.	Newsprint, marker
Investigation of Betrayal	12 to 15	REALITY CHECK—Form groups to compare anonymous, real-life stories of betrayal with experiences in their own lives.	"Profiles of Betrayal" handouts (p. 20), highlighter pens, newsprint, marker, tape
	3 to 5	WHO BETRAYED WHOM?—Guess the identities of the people profiled in the handouts.	Paper, tape, pen
Investigation of True Love	15 to 18	SOURCE WORK—Study and discuss God's definition of perfect love.	Bibles, newsprint, marker
	5 to 7	LOVE MESSAGES—Create unique ways to send a "message of love" to the victims of betrayal they've been studying.	Newsprint, markers, tape
Personal Application	10 to 15	SYMBOLIC LOVE—Give a partner a personal symbol of perfect love.	Paper lunch sack, pens, scissors, paper, catalogs

notes:

● **A Relevant Topic**—More than ever before, kids live in the now. What matters to them and what attracts their hearts is what's happening in their world at this moment. For this reason, every Core Belief Bible Study focuses on a particular hot topic that kids care about.

● **A Core Christian Belief**—Group's Core Belief Bible Study Series organizes the wealth of Christian truth and experience into twenty-four Core Christian Belief categories. These twenty-four headings act as umbrellas for a collection of detailed beliefs that define Christianity and set it apart from the world and every other religion. Each book in this series features one Core Christian Belief with lessons suited for junior high or senior high students.

"But," you ask, "won't my kids be bored talking about all these spiritual beliefs?" No way! As a youth leader, you know the value of using hot topics to connect with young people. Ultimately teenagers talk about issues because they're searching for meaning in their lives. They want to find the one equation that will make sense of all the confusing events happening around them. Each Core Belief Bible Study answers that need by connecting a hot topic with a powerful Christian principle. Kids walk away from the study with something more solid than just the shifting ebb and flow of their own opinions. They walk away with a deeper understanding of their Christian faith.

● **The Point**—This simple statement is designed to be the intersection between the Core Christian Belief and the hot topic. Everything in the study ultimately focuses on The Point so that kids study it and allow it time to sink into their hearts.

● **The Study at a Glance**—A quick look at this chart will tell you what kids will do, how long it will take them to do it, and what supplies you'll need to get it done.

● **The Bible Connection**—This is the power base of each study. Whether it's just one verse or several chapters, The Bible Connection provides the vital link between kids' minds and their hearts. The content of each Core Belief Bible Study reflects the belief that the true power of God—the power to expose, heal, and change kids' lives—is contained in his Word.

THE POINT OF *BETRAYED!*:

God is love.

THE BIBLE CONNECTION

1 JOHN 4:7-21  The Apostle John explains the nature and definition of perfect love.

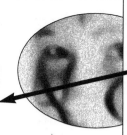

In this study, kids will compare the imperfect love defined in real-life stories of betrayal to God's definition of perfect love.

By making this comparison, kids can discover that God is love and therefore incapable of betraying them. Then they'll be able to recognize the incredible opportunity God offers to experience the only relationship worthy of their absolute trust.

Explore the verses in The Bible Connect[ion] mation in the Depthfinder boxes throughout understanding of how these Scriptures con[nect]

LEADER TIP for The Study

Because this topic can be so powerful and relevant to kids' lives, your group members may be tempted to get caught up in issues and lose sight of the deeper biblical principle found in The Point. Help your kids grasp The Point by guiding kids to focus on the biblical investigation and discussing how God's truth connects with reality in their lives.

THE STUDY

DISCUSSION STARTER ▼

Jump-Start (up to 5 minutes) As kids arrive, ask them to thi[nk of] common themes in movies, books, TV sho[ws] have kids each contribute ideas for a mas[ter list] two other kids in the room and sharing [their] sider providing copies of People mag[azine to] what's currently showing on television or at [the...] their suggestions, write their respo[nses on ne...] **come up with a lot of great ide[as. Even th...] ent, look through this list an[d] try to disc[over...] ments most of these theme[s] have in com[mon.]**

After kids make several s[ug]gestions, menti[on...] responses are connected w[ith] the idea of bet[rayal.]

● **Why do you think [b]etrayal is such a [...]**

Betrayed! **17**

DEPTHFINDER UNDERSTANDING INTEGRITY

Your students may not be entirely familiar with the meaning of integrity, especially as it might apply to God's character in the Trinity. Use these definitions (taken from Webster's II New Riverside Dictionary) and other information to help you guide kids toward a better understanding of how God maintains integrity through the three expressions of the Trinity.

Integrity: 1. Firm adherence to a code or standard of values. 2. The state of being unimpaired. 3. The quality or condition of being undivided.

Synonyms for integrity include probity, completeness, wholeness, soundness, and perfection.

Our word "integrity" comes from the Latin word *integritas*, which means soundness. *Integritas* is also the root of the word "integer," which means "whole or complete," as in a "whole" number.

The Hebrew word that's often translated "integrity" (for example, in Psalm 25:21 [NIV]) is *tam*. It means whole, perfect, sincere, and honest.

CREATIVE GOD-EXPLORATION ▼

Top Hats (18 to 20 minutes) Form three groups, with each trio member from the previous activity going to a different group. Give each group Bibles, paper, and pens, and assign each group a different hat God wears: Father, Son, or Holy Spirit.

[...] their goal is to write one list describing what God does in the [...] God's character.

● **Depthfinder Boxes**— These informative sidelights located throughout each study add insight into a particular passage, word, historical fact, or Christian doctrine. Depthfinder boxes also provide insight into teen culture, adolescent development, current events, and philosophy.

● **Leader Tips**— These handy information boxes coach you through the study, offering helpful suggestions on everything from altering activities for different-sized groups to streamlining discussions to using effective discipline techniques.

H o l y P r o f i l e s

handout

Your assigned Bible passage describes how a particular person or group responded when confronted with God's holiness. Use the information in your passage to help your group discuss the questions below. Then use your flashlights to teach the other two groups what you discover.

■ Based on your passage, what does holiness look like?

■ What does holiness sound like?

■ When people see God's holiness, how does it affect them?

■ How is this response to God's holiness like humility?

■ Based on your passage, how would you describe humility?

■ Why is humility an appropriate human response to God's holiness?

■ Based on what you see in your passage, do you think you are a humble person? Why or why not?

■ What's one way you could develop humility in your life this week?

● **Handouts**—Most Core Belief Bible Studies include photocopiable handouts to use with your group. Handouts might take the form of a fun game, a lively discussion starter, or a challenging study page for kids to take home— anything to make your study more meaningful and effective.

The Last Word on Core Belief Bible Studies

Soon after you begin to use Group's Core Belief Bible Study Series, you'll see signs of real growth in your group members. Your kids will gain a deeper understanding of the Bible and of their own Christian faith. They'll see more clearly how a relationship with Jesus affects their daily lives. And they'll grow closer to God.

But that's not all. You'll also see kids grow closer to one another.

That's because this series is founded on the principle that Christian faith grows best in the context of relationship. Each study uses a variety of interactive pairs and small groups and always includes discussion questions that promote deeper relationships. The friendships kids will build through this study series will enable them to grow *together* toward a deeper relationship with God.

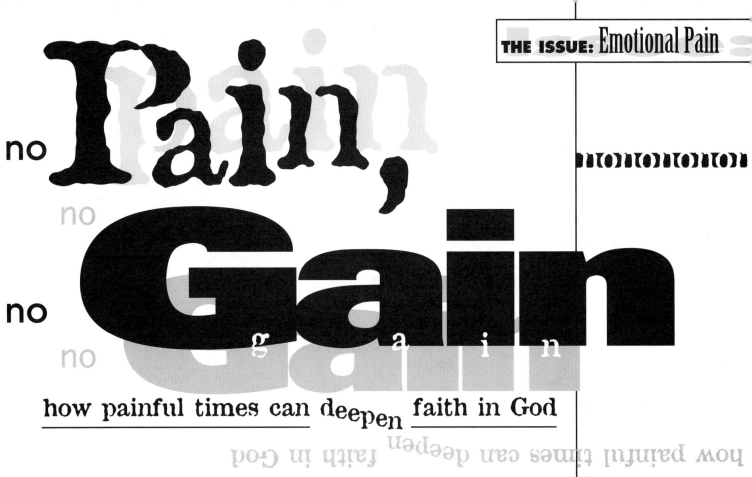

no Pain, no Gain

how painful times can deepen faith in God

how painful times can deepen faith in God

by Michael D. Warden

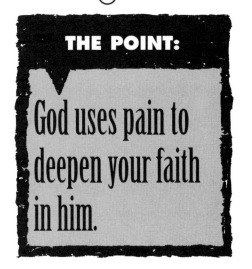

THE POINT:

God uses pain to deepen your faith in him.

■ "Look, it's nuthin'. No big deal. I'm fine." ■ They may be called a generation of complainers, but try to get most kids to talk about their hurts, and that's the response you'll get most often—"Nothing's wrong. Nuthin'." ■ Maybe this "lone wolf" attitude of today's teenagers is just a reaction to being labeled as whiners. Maybe they're afraid their pain will make them too vulnerable. Or maybe they just aren't sure who they can really trust. Whatever their reasons, one thing is sure—their pain matters to God. ■ This study probes deeply into the hidden places in kids' lives—in an attempt to uncover their pain and help them discover how God can work through their hurts to create something beautiful.

The Study
AT A GLANCE

SECTION	MINUTES	WHAT STUDENTS WILL DO	SUPPLIES
Creative Project	5 to 10	DREAM SHAPES—Cut poster board into the shape of a dream.	Poster board, scissors, Bible
Learning Journey	5 to 10	PREP TIME—Form trios to prepare for their learning journeys.	
	30 to 40	PAIN PORTRAITS—Travel to different stations in the room and work within trios to create personal pain portraits.	"Joseph's Journey" handouts (p. 22), paper, construction paper, scissors, pens, Bibles, transparent tape, markers, pitcher of ice water, paper cups
Final Station	5 to 10	JOURNEY'S END—Create a symbol or drawing of a painful situation in their lives, then pray about it with others.	Bibles, paper, construction paper, scissors, pens, tape, markers

notes:

God uses pain to deepen your faith in him.

THE BIBLE CONNECTION

GENESIS 37:1-11, 17b-36; 39:1-20; 40:1-23; 41:1-43   These passages describe events in Joseph's life.

In this study, kids will go on a "journey" to examine the pain in Joseph's life and uncover connections between his experiences and their own.

Through this journey, kids will discover how God can use the pain in their own lives to deepen their relationship with Jesus.

Explore the verses in The Bible Connection, then study the information in the Depthfinder boxes throughout the study to gain a deeper understanding of how these Scriptures connect with your young people.

LEADER TIP
for The Study

Whenever you tell groups to discuss a list of questions, write the questions on newsprint and tape the newsprint to the wall so groups can discuss the questions at their own pace.

BEFORE THE STUDY

Follow these steps to set up your meeting area for the journey kids will take:

1. Set up three tables at different places in the meeting room. Leave enough space around each table to allow kids to spread out on the floor and work. If your meeting room is small, or if you expect more than twelve kids, consider holding this study in a larger room or even the church sanctuary.

2. Label the tables "Station 1," "Station 2," and "Station 3."

3. At Station 1, set out paper, pens, scissors, markers, construction paper, transparent tape, and copies of the "Station 1" section of the "Joseph's Journey" handout (p. 22).

4. At Station 2, set out tape and copies of the "Station 2" section of the "Joseph's Journey" handout (p. 22).

5. At Station 3, set out a pitcher of ice water, small paper cups, markers, tape, and copies of the "Station 3" section of the "Joseph's Journey" handout (p. 23).

THE STUDY

CREATIVE PROJECT ▼

Dream Shapes (5 to 10 minutes)

As students arrive, give each a sheet of poster board and scissors. Once everyone is present, read aloud Genesis 37:1-11. Tell kids to cut their sheets of poster board into the shape of a dream they have for their lives. For example, a football shape might represent a dream to play professional ball, or a book shape might represent a dream to become a writer. Kids can make any shapes they want, but encourage them to leave plenty of space to write on them. Kids will use these later as the "blank canvas" for their "pain portraits."

As they finish, have kids turn to partners and use their dream shapes to each tell about one great dream they have for their lives. Then say: **Sometimes the dreams we have are planted in us by God to help us understand his plan for our lives. But even when our dreams are from God, that doesn't mean achieving them will be easy or painless. Following your dream may cause you to hurt in ways you can't foresee now. The good news is that God can use your setbacks and disappointments to help you grow closer to him.**

Today we'll use Joseph's life story to explore the emotional pain we all feel and discover ways <u>God uses that pain to deepen our faith in him.</u>

DEPTHFINDER UNDERSTANDING THE BIBLE

Joseph was the eleventh of Jacob's twelve sons and the firstborn son of Rachel. He probably lived sometime between 1720 and 1550 B.C., during the reign of the Hyksos pharaohs (naturalized Egyptians whose ancestors were Semitic slaves from Canaan). Joseph eventually became the ancestor of two of the twelve Jewish tribes, Manasseh and Ephraim.

Through the story of his life recorded in Genesis, Joseph presents a noble ideal of godly character. Though confronted with betrayal, isolation, and the loss of personal dignity, Joseph was consistently gentle, forgiving, and faithful to God. These qualities so remarkably convey the essence of godliness that Joseph is often regarded as an Old Testament type of Christ.

Prep Time (5 to 10 minutes)

Form trios, and have kids in each trio choose one of these roles: Reader (reads aloud all the Bible passages assigned), Questioner (asks all the questions from the handout), and Team Leader (keeps the trio on course and encourages everyone to participate). Then say: **You're about to go on a learning journey with your two partners. Your goal in this journey is to use your dream shape to create a "personal pain portrait" that highlights some of the pain you've felt in your life and then discover how God might use that pain to deepen your faith in him.**

Your trio will examine the events in Joseph's life by going to each station in order and following the instructions provided there. As you study your assigned passages, look for ways God used pain in Joseph's life to deepen his faith. See if you can discover how God might use pain in your own life in a similar way.

When trios are ready, pray: **Lord, guide us through this journey, and help us understand why you allow us to hurt sometimes. In Jesus' name, amen.**

Start trios on their journeys.

Pain Portraits (30 to 40 minutes)

As trios begin, walk around the room and write on each pain portrait one positive quality you see in that person that you think has come as the result of struggle in life. For example, you might write "patience" for someone who's endured a difficult relationship or "great sense of humor" for someone who's learned to laugh through hard times. If your group is large, ask an adult volunteer to help with this assignment. Make sure no one is left out.

In addition to writing affirmations, make yourself available to help kids study Bible passages, create symbols, or discuss how Joseph's circumstances might relate to their own.

Because trios will complete Station 3 at different times, use these suggestions to help trios fill the time while they wait for the rest of the class to finish:

● Have students take a quick timeout from their trios and find new partners. Have kids explain their pain portraits to these new partners, then return to their trios.

● As trios complete the third station, have them move off to the side and prepare for the final station by reading together Genesis 41:1-43.

LEADER TIP for Pain Portraits

To create a thoughtful atmosphere in the room, drape colored sheets over the windows and place several lit candles at each station. In addition, play soft music in the background while students work on their projects.

Journey's End (5 to 10 minutes)

When all the trios have finished Station 3, gather everyone together on the floor. Say: **In a moment we'll complete our pain portraits. But first let's see what happened to Joseph at the end of his struggles.**

LEADER TIP

for The Study

Because this topic can be so powerful and relevant to kids' lives, your group members may be tempted to get caught up in issues and lose sight of the deeper biblical principle found in The Point. Help your kids grasp The Point by guiding them to focus on the biblical investigation and by discussing how God's truth connects with reality in their lives.

DEPTH FINDER
UNDERSTANDING THE BIBLE

Your kids may wonder why a loving God would allow them to feel pain at all. According to the Bible, emotional pain comes into our lives for a variety of reasons. Here's a sampling: Emotional pain comes

● as the result of sinful actions (Galatians 6:8),

● as God's discipline to correct us when we step out of his will (Proverbs 3:12),

● to test us or purify our hearts and make us more like Jesus (Psalm 66:10 and James 1:2-3), or

● to compel us toward a deeper relationship with God (Psalm 119:67 and Romans 8:35-37).

Whatever the cause for emotional pain, one truth remains constant—God can use pain for our good (Romans 8:28).

Have volunteers read aloud Genesis 41:1-8, 14-16, 25-28, and 39-40. Then ask:

● **Why did God allow Joseph to go through so much pain before letting his dream come true?**

● **Was Joseph's pain essential to his success later? Why or why not?**

● **Is your present pain a necessary part of your future success? Why or why not?**

Using the supplies from Station 1, have each student create a symbol, write a paragraph, or create a drawing that represents a pain he or she is experiencing right now. When kids are finished, have them explain their symbols to their trios. Have trios pray together, asking God to show them how the pain in their lives can deepen their faith in him.

As trios finish praying, challenge them by saying: **Keep your personal pain portraits on a wall in your bedroom until you've prayed about each of your "pain times" to discover how God can help you deepen your faith in him.**

TEEN
opinion

We went online to get young people's responses to this question: "What do you do to help you get through painful times?" Here's what some of them said:

from: Littlelolo

I go online and go out with friends—anything to get my mind off my troubles and get out of the house, which is usually where the trouble is.

from: SykoPyro

Several things that sometimes help me are typing e-mail to a few of my closest friends whom I trust. I also find it helpful to do free-writing when I'm upset or depressed. I often end up explaining to myself what's wrong and it helps me to organize my life. Poetry is also sometimes a good outlet for my emotions.

from: Dream 4EVR

Dear SykoPyro, I use the same technique a lot. Unfortunately, once I tried writing a story about a girl like me and I had to stop because it made me suicidal.

from: Scaroovie

I think the best way to put up with all the [trouble] that people and the world give you is just to look really [angry] all the time. I learned this by going to school and constantly hearing about how fat and ugly and stupid I was. Now I just look [angry] and no one messes with me any more.

from: Samsman1

What I do is listen to music, Nirvana especially. Don't ask me why that helps. I don't have a clue.

Joseph's
J o u r n e y

Photocopy and cut apart these sections, then place each set of instructions at the appropriate station. Make enough copies of each set so everyone can have one.

STATION 1
Instructions
1. Read the story of Joseph's betrayal by his brothers in Genesis 37:17b-36.
2. Discuss these questions:
● If you were with Joseph down in the well, what would you say to him?
● Have you ever felt betrayed by a family member? Explain.
● How can the pain of family betrayal strengthen your faith in God?
3. Use the supplies to create a symbol, write a paragraph, or draw a picture that describes a time you felt betrayed by someone in your family. Attach your creation to your pain portrait, and write "Genesis 37:17b-36" next to it.
4. Explain your symbol to your trio.

Move on to Station 2.

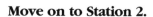

STATION 2
Instructions
1. Read how Potiphar's wife destroyed Joseph's reputation in Genesis 39:1-20.
2. Choose something you have on to represent a time when someone misunderstood you or deliberately tried to hurt you. For example, a shoestring might represent how someone tried to "trip you up" by spreading rumors about you. Explain your symbol to your trio, then use tape to attach it to your pain portrait. Next to the item write "Genesis 39:1-20."
3. Discuss these questions:
● How is removing something you're wearing like losing a "piece" of your dignity and self-respect?
● In Joseph's encounter with Potiphar's wife, he lost far more than just his clothes. He lost his dignity. When have you felt like someone was trying to rob you of your dignity?
● How can an experience like the one you described help deepen your faith in God?

Move on to Station 3.

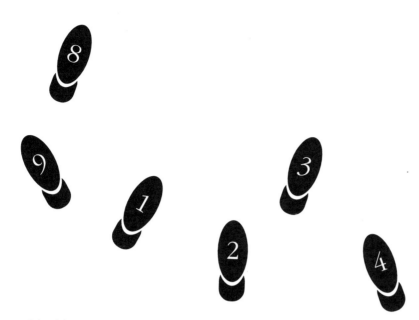

STATION 3
Instructions

1. Read how Joseph's friend forgot about him in Genesis 40:1-23.

2. Discuss these questions:

● After this incident, Joseph spent two more years in prison before anyone remembered him. How would you have felt in Joseph's place?

● If you were Joseph, what would you have said to God?

3. Fill three cups with ice water. Take turns letting one partner pour ice water into your mouth while the other partner holds your arms to your sides.

4. Discuss these questions:

● How is this experience like trusting God in painful times?

● How can friends make a difference when you're hurting?

5. On each partner's cup write one quality that makes that person a good friend to have during painful times. When everyone is finished, attach your cup to your pain portrait. Next to the cup write "Genesis 40:1-23."

Ask your leader for further instructions.

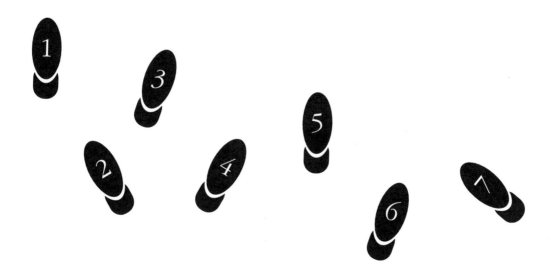

Taking a Stand
What Motivates Young People to Stand Up for Christ

by Michael D. Warden

■ Kids today are caught in a cross-fire of contradictory beliefs. Having listened to their elders preach about respect for diversity in culture and religion, young people have responded by adopting an "anything goes" attitude toward faith: "Believe whatever you like," they say, "just don't push it on anyone else." ■ But under these surface thoughts pulses a different conviction that fights to break free. Raised in a culture of mediocrity, today's kids secretly long to live boldly—to believe in something enough to sacrifice anything for it. And if necessary, even to die for their cause. ■ This study focuses on God's love as the purest motivation for personal sacrifice, and encourages kids to recognize that their relationship with Jesus is worth the sacrificial suffering he calls all Christians to embrace.

THE POINT:

Your relationship with Jesus is worth suffering for.

The Study
AT A GLANCE

SECTION	MINUTES	WHAT STUDENTS WILL DO	SUPPLIES
Relational Exploration	5 to 7	STAND FOR SOMEONE—Stand in an uncomfortable position while discussing who they'd be willing to suffer for.	"Quotes" handouts (p. 31)
	5 to 7	OUTSTANDING COMMITMENTS—Label themselves with the names of people they'd suffer for.	Index cards, pens, tape
Three-Way Investigation	18 to 20	FOR THE SAKE OF LOVE—Form three groups to explore different aspects of suffering for Christ.	Bibles, assorted magazines, construction paper, tape, markers, newsprint, assorted scrap items, paper, pencils
	7 to 10	WHY SUFFER?—Find creative ways to teach the other groups what they learned.	Bibles, "Love and Suffering" handouts (p. 33)
Commitment	10 to 15	TOKENS OF LOVE—Make a symbol that represents a relationship they'd be willing to suffer for.	16-gauge copper wire, wire cutters or scissors

notes:

Your relationship with Jesus is worth suffering for.

THE BIBLE CONNECTION

ROMANS 5:1-5; 2 CORINTHIANS 11:21-29; PHILIPPIANS 3:7-11; 2 TIMOTHY 1:8-12	Paul talks about suffering for Jesus and its rewards.
MATTHEW 5:10-12	Jesus blesses those followers who suffer because of their faith.
1 PETER 4:12-19	Peter admonishes Christians to be ready to suffer for doing good.

I n this study, kids will compare the Apostle Paul's willingness to suffer for Christ with their own attitudes about suffering and explore how deeply they value their faith in God.

By making this comparison, kids can discover the overwhelming value of knowing and following Jesus and recognize their own capacity for godly self-sacrifice.

Explore the verses in The Bible Connection, then examine the information in the Depthfinder boxes throughout the study to gain a deeper understanding of how these Scriptures connect with your young people.

BEFORE THE STUDY

Set up three stations for the "For the Sake of Love" activity in different areas of the room. At the first station, you'll need a stack of assorted magazines, colored construction paper, tape, markers, newsprint, and assorted junk items such as old clothes, shoes, or hats. At the second station, you'll need the same supplies you provided at the first station. At the third station, you'll need paper and pencils.

Make one photocopy of the "Love and Suffering" handout (p. 33) for each student.

Cut one two-foot length of 16-gauge copper wire for each student.

LEADER TIP for The Study

Because this topic can be so powerful and relevant to kids' lives, your group members may be tempted to get caught up in issues and lose sight of the deeper biblical principle found in The Point. Help your kids grasp The Point by guiding them to focus on the biblical investigation and by discussing how God's truth connects with reality in their lives.

THE STUDY

RELATIONAL EXPLORATION ▼

Stand for Someone (5 to 7 minutes)
As kids arrive, hold up the "Quotes" handout (p. 31) and have them read the short quips about the real-life people. Then have them turn to partners and discuss this question:

● **What does "taking a stand" for something or someone mean to you?**

Once everyone has arrived, form groups of four. Have each group member form a cross with his or her body, standing with arms outstretched. Tell group members to hold this position as they discuss these questions:

● **Who in your life are you willing to stand up for?**
● **What's the benefit of standing up for someone you care about?**
● **Who in your life are you willing to suffer for if necessary?**
● **What's the benefit of suffering for someone you care about?**

After the discussion, allow kids to lower their arms.

Outstanding Commitments (5 to 7 minutes)
In their groups, have kids discuss these questions:

● **How did it feel to hold your arms in that position for so long?**
● **How is that feeling like the way it feels to suffer for someone you care about? How is it different?**

Give each student an index card, a pen, and some tape. Say: **On your card, write the name of one person you said you'd be willing to suffer for. Then tape that name over your heart.**

When kids have done this, gather them all together and ask:

● **How does it feel to wear that name over your heart?**
● **I can tell you all care about the people whose names you wrote on your cards. Does loving someone mean you should be willing to stand up for them? Why or why not?**
● **Does loving them mean you should be willing to suffer for them? Why or why not?**

Tell kids you want them to wear their cards for the rest of the study as a sign of their commitment to stand up for someone they love. Then say: **Today we're going to talk about suffering—not the kind of suffering that happens when you break your leg, catch a disease, or go to prison for committing a crime. We're going to talk about the kind of suffering that comes because you love somebody. In particular, we're going to explore what part suffering plays in your relationship with Jesus. Our goal is to see how valuable Jesus is and recognize that <u>your relationship with him is worth suffering for.</u>**

LEADER TIP

for Stand for Someone

You may want to list the discussion questions on newsprint so groups can respond to the questions at their own pace. Also, kids will become tired during this discussion and may want to lower their arms. Sympathize with their discomfort, but encourage kids to keep their arms fully raised until their group is finished.

DEPTHFINDER UNDERSTANDING THESE KIDS

In this study on godly suffering, is it appropriate to tell kids, "Since Jesus died for you, you should be willing to suffer for him"? Before answering yes or no, consider what young people may hear when asked that question.

Today's Christian teenagers typically don't view their faith as a "righteous cause" they must defend. They see it more as a *personal relationship* they must pursue. While sacrificing for a just cause may be noble, sacrificing for a relationship is a far more personal matter. Because of this, your kids may perceive a "third party's" challenge to "suffer for the cause of Christ" as personally invasive or simply as an attempt at guilt manipulation.

Your kids probably won't suffer for Christ just because it's "the right thing to do"; they'll suffer for Christ because they *love* him.

THREE-WAY INVESTIGATION ▼

For the Sake of Love (18 to 20 minutes)

Form three groups. Then say: **If we examine how other people have suffered for Christ and how that suffering impacted their lives, you can discover how your relationship with Jesus is worth suffering for.**  Tell kids that they're going to conduct a three-way investigation to explore how the Apostle Paul suffered for following Christ, and they'll compare that to the lives of people in their own church. Their goal is to decide for themselves whether Jesus is really worth suffering for.

Number the groups from one to three, then assign each an "investigative task" according to these instructions:

Group 1—Gather these kids in one corner of the meeting room.

Say: **Your goal is to make this corner of the room look like Paul's suffering.**

Assign kids these passages to study: 2 Corinthians 11:21-29; Philippians 3:7-11; and 2 Timothy 1:8-12. As kids read these passages, have them look for specific ways Paul suffered for Christ. Then encourage kids to use the supplies you've provided to transform their corner of the room to reflect what they discover.

Group 2—Gather these kids in a different corner of the meeting room.

Say: **Your goal is to make this corner of the room look like what Paul gained from suffering for Christ.**

Assign kids these passages to study: Matthew 5:10-12; Romans 5:1-5; Philippians 3:7-11; and 1 Peter 4:12-19. As kids read these passages, have them look for specific ways Paul benefited from suffering for Christ. Then encourage kids to use the supplies you've provided to transform their corner of the room to reflect what they discover.

Group 3—Gather this group near the door of the meeting room. Have kids form pairs, then say: **Your goal is to discover how much people in our church are willing to suffer for Christ.**

Tell kids to go out in pairs, find at least three people, and ask them each this question:

LEADER TIP

for For the Sake of Love

Before sending Group 3 out to interview, talk to adult leaders in your church to arrange permission for kids to "drop in" on specific adult groups that won't mind the interruption.

If your group meets when no adults are around, provide kids with a list of adults' phone numbers and have kids conduct the interviews by phone.

DEPTHFINDER   UNDERSTANDING THESE KIDS

As your young people examine Paul's view of suffering, they may be tempted to dismiss his words because they think the persecution he experienced doesn't happen to Christians anymore—especially in the United States. But that's not the truth. In fact, right now there are Christians in this country and all over the world who are suffering for their faith. Many of these will even be tortured and killed for what they believe.

To help kids "connect" with Christian suffering in the modern world, consider having them receive a free subscription to Voice of the Martyrs, a newsletter that tracks Christian persecution across the globe. For a free subscription, write P.O. Box 443, Bartlesville, OK 74005, or call (918) 337-8015.

● **To what degree would you be willing to suffer for your faith in Christ?**

Have kids record people's responses on their papers. After they've each interviewed at least three people, have them return to the meeting room.

LEADER TIP
for Why Suffer?

As a part of the debriefing process, consider providing kids a photocopy of the Depthfinder entitled "The Bible vs. the Western World" (p. 32). The points in the Depthfinder may spur even deeper discussion about suffering and the Christian faith!

Why Suffer? (7 to 10 minutes)

When all the groups have completed their investigations, instruct each group to prepare a brief creative presentation of its discoveries for the other groups. Allow groups to present their information however they want, as long as each member of the group participates in some way. Encourage creativity. For example, kids from one group might present their discoveries by taking the class on a tour of its "Museum of Suffering," while another group might present an on-the-spot "Readers Theater," in which each person reads quotes from the adult interviews on suffering. When groups are ready, have them each present their information.

After the presentations, call everyone together, and congratulate kids on their efforts. Distribute copies of the "Love and Suffering" handout (p. 33). Have kids form pairs and go through the discussion questions together. Every few minutes, have pairs report back to the whole group about what they're discussing.

After the discussion, say: **People throughout the centuries have often been willing to suffer for a "cause" or an ideal. Many have even been willing to die. But suffering for a person isn't a matter of ideals—it's a matter of love. Your relationship with Jesus is worth suffering for, because he loves you more than anyone else ever could.**

COMMITMENT ▼

Tokens of Love (10 to 15 minutes)

Have each person remove the card taped over his or her heart and look at the name written on it. Say: **When we're willing** to suffer for someone we love, that makes us all a little like Jesus. He was willing to suffer for us—he even died—because he loves us.

As a celebration of this Christlike quality in you, I'd like us all to participate in a group challenge!

Give each student a two-foot length of 16-gauge copper wire (this wire can be purchased cheaply at any hardware store). Instruct kids to shape the wire into a symbol that represents the person they each named on their cards at the beginning of the study.

When kids have finished, say: **Now, here's the challenge. For the next week, take your symbol with you wherever you go. If possible, wear it around your neck or keep it in your wallet. At various times during the week, tell at least five different people what the symbol stands for and why you'd be willing to suffer for the person it represents. Make sure at least one of those five people is the actual person the symbol stands for.**

Close the study by having kids form pairs and explain their copper symbols to their partners. Then have partners pray together for God to deepen their love for him.

LEADER TIP
for Tokens of Love

If you prefer not to use the copper wire for this activity, you can substitute string instead. Just have kids shape the string into a symbol and use clear tape to secure it to an index card.

"Quotes"

Charlynn Rohr, student—
stands up for Christ by committing to remain a virgin until marriage.

Lori Fliestra, student—
stands up for Christ by selling her artwork to support needy children in New Mexico.

A.C. Green, basketball player—
stands up for Christ by challenging kids to save sex for marriage.

Common Western Belief	The Bible
If it feels good, it must be right for you. Conversely, if it feels bad, it must be wrong for you.	"We also have joy with our troubles, because we know that these troubles produce patience. And patience produces character, and character produces hope" (Romans 5:3-4).
You shouldn't have to suffer.	"People will insult you and hurt you. They will lie and say all kinds of evil things about you because you follow me. But when they do, you will be happy. Rejoice and be glad, because you have a great reward waiting for you in heaven" (Matthew 5:11-12a).
Suffering is bad.	"My brothers and sisters, when you have many kinds of troubles you should be full of joy, because you know that these troubles test your faith, and this will give you patience" (James 1:2-3).
If you're suffering, then something is wrong with you or your life.	"My friends, do not be surprised at the terrible trouble which now comes to test you. Do not think that something strange is happening to you. But be happy that you are sharing in Christ's sufferings so that you will be happy and full of joy when Christ comes again in glory" (1 Peter 4:12-13).
You should never parade your beliefs and make someone else uncomfortable.	"You are the light that gives light to the world. A city that is built on a hill cannot be hidden" (Matthew 5:14).
Everyone suffers. Nevertheless, you should do all you can to avoid suffering in your life.	"Do not suffer for murder, theft, or any other crime, nor because you trouble other people. But if you suffer because you are a Christian, do not be ashamed. Praise God because you wear that name" (1 Peter 4:15-16).

Use the discussion questions below to continue your investigation into whether your relationship with Jesus is worth suffering for.

1. What did you learn from these investigations?

2. Read Philippians 3:7-11. What surprises you most about Paul's attitude toward suffering for Christ?

3. How do you think love is related to suffering?

4. Read 1 Peter 4:12-19. What surprises you most about your church members' attitudes toward suffering for Christ?

5. Is the "willingness to suffer" a good measure of how much you love someone? Why or why not?

6. What did Paul hope to gain by suffering for Christ?

7. Read Matthew 5:10-12. What qualities do you see in Jesus that would make him worth suffering for?

8. What would suffering for Christ look like in the modern world?

9. If you were to suffer for Christ, what do you think you would gain from it? Explain.

10. Read 2 Timothy 2:8-13. Are you willing to suffer for your relationship with Jesus? Why or why not?

Pause for a few moments to pray together. Ask God to strengthen your faith and help you to deepen your love for him. After you pray, complete the discussion by responding to these questions:

11. Read Romans 5:6-8. What qualities do you see in the person across from you that would make Christ willing to suffer for him or her?

12. Does knowing that Jesus suffered for you help you believe that he's worth suffering for? Why or why not?

TORN in TWO

Helping Kids Cope With Family Crises

by Karl Leuthauser

THE POINT:

God is with you when you hurt.

■ In his book *Children at Risk,* Dr. James Dobson warns that "nothing short of a great Civil War of Values rages throughout North America." In the same book, Gary L. Bauer explains that "more than one million children are affected by divorce every year. Mates are traded in for newer models as if they were cars." And so the battle rages on. We fight to preserve the traditional family because we, like God, hate the pain that is caused by tearing apart those he has joined. ■ But more than we hate divorce, we must love those who have been broken because of it: the children, the single parents, the impoverished, the isolated, and the rejected. ■ This study will help your kids to see that God is with them as they face the hurt that inevitably comes with a broken home. It encourages them to work for the best possible relationships with their family members despite imperfect circumstances. It will challenge kids to honor their parents regardless of the mistakes they've made.

The Study
AT A GLANCE

SECTION	MINUTES	WHAT STUDENTS WILL DO	SUPPLIES
Interactive Role-Play	20 to 30	WARD AND JUNE—Create perfect families and present responses to family crises.	"Ward and June" handout (p. 44)
Creative Options	15 to 20	IT HAPPENS—Demonstrate four different creative responses to a case study.	Bibles, "God Is With You" handout (p. 45), paper, pencils, newsprint, a marker
Learning Puzzle	10 to 15	CLIP ART—Solve a symbolic puzzle made from paper clips.	Bibles, paper clips, masking tape, a pencil

notes:

God is with you when you hurt.

THE BIBLE CONNECTION

PSALM 23	God is with us in times of trouble.
PSALM 40:1-3; 120:1	God will hear and answer us when we look to him for help.
EPHESIANS 6:1-3	God wants us to honor our parents.

I n this study, kids will create model families and have their families respond to various family crises. They'll hear a case study about divorce and have an opportunity to react to the situation. They'll conclude the study by solving a puzzle that helps them understand how family members function during a divorce.

By doing this, kids can learn that regardless of how broken their family is, God is with them when they hurt. They can discover that with God's help, they can honor their parents, even if they live in a broken home.

Explore the verses in The Bible Connection, then examine the information in the Depthfinder boxes throughout the study to gain a deeper understanding of how these Scriptures connect with your young people.

LEADER TIP
for The Study

Whenever groups discuss a list of questions, write the questions on newsprint and tape the newsprint to a wall so groups can discuss the questions at their own pace.

BEFORE THE STUDY

Make one paper clip puzzle for each student in your group.
Follow the directions on page 42 to make the puzzles.

THE STUDY

THE STUDY

INTERACTIVE ROLE-PLAY ▼

Ward and June

(20 to 30 minutes)

As kids arrive, have them form groups of four. Try to have at least one guy and one girl in every group. Say: **I'd like each group to come up with a definition of the perfect family. Please discuss these questions in your groups to help you:**

- **How many people would a perfect family have?**
- **What roles would each of the members of a perfect family play?**
- **How would a perfect family make decisions?**
- **How would the family spend time together?**
- **Would the family have arguments? If so, what would they argue about? How would they resolve their arguments?**
- **How would a perfect family be different from other families?**

When kids finish, say: **I'd like each group to create a perfect family. Do this by assigning each of the roles for your perfect family to the members of your group. For example, if you decided that a perfect family has a mother, a father, and two kids, have one person fill each one of those roles.** While kids come up with their perfect families, give each group one of the situations found on the "Ward

LEADER TIP
for Ward and June

To make the role-play more interesting, provide props for your students to use. Put the props in the center of the room, and let students use any or all of the props as they present their families' responses. Some prop ideas include hats, wigs, jackets, ties, shoes, an empty box of matches, and a ball.

LEADER TIP
for Ward and June

If a group has more participants than roles, give the group a long piece of twine or yarn. Have extra group members tie themselves together at the waist and act as a single family member. If a group has more roles than participants, have one or more students double up on roles. Ask students to show the different characters by changing their voices and switching props (if provided).

DEPTH FINDER — SUPPORTING SINGLE PARENTS

Chances are that a few kids in your group come from single-parent families. Unfortunately, many churches and Christians have unintentionally caused these kids and their parents to feel like second-class citizens in the Christian community. Here are ten ways that you can reverse the damage done by reaching out to and supporting single-parent families:

- **Pray** for wisdom about what to say. Listen and be available.
- **Reach** out to the children. Invite them on outings or to church.
- **Offer practical help** such as free baby-sitting, yard work, car or plumbing repairs, etc. Cook a meal—set a date and follow through.
- **Invite** single friends to dinner, and don't forget holidays and birthdays.
- **Reaffirm** their self-worth—accept and uplift.
- **Empathize.** Put yourself in their place.
- **Encourage** them to visit their pastor for counsel.
- **Contact**—cards, notes, poems, Bible verses, phone calls.
- **Take them somewhere normal and fun**—a picnic, a ball game, a church program, or the gym.
- **Fellowship.** Invite them to join your Bible study or Christian support group; introduce them to a single-parents fellowship group.

(Mike Yorkey, ed., *Growing a Healthy Home*)

and June" handout (p. 44).

Say: **I've just given you a situation that your perfect family must face. Take the next few minutes to decide how you're going to act out that situation for everyone else. Make sure you present the situation so everyone can understand what's going on. Make sure you show how your perfect family would react.**

Give groups about five minutes to prepare. Then ask each group to present its situation and the family's response. After everyone has had a chance to present, have the groups discuss the following questions:

● **Would your real family respond to the situation in the same way that your group's perfect family responded? Explain.**

● **What's the most important thing that would need to change for your real family to be almost perfect?**

● **What's the best thing about being a member of your family?**

● **What's the hardest thing about being part of your family?**

● **How are most families different from your group's model of a perfect family?**

Then say: **Families are gifts from God. They're designed to offer protection, support, and love for us as we grow. There is no such thing as a perfect family. Unfortunately, the imperfections that every family has can cause serious pain in the lives of family members. A divorce, a fight, or even a careless comment can cause hurt. Fortunately, <u>God is with you when you hurt.</u>**

LEADER TIP for Ward and June

If you don't have enough guys or girls to put at least one member of each sex in every group, don't worry. Just have girls speak in low voices and guys speak in high voices as they act out opposite-sex roles. This arrangement can produce some humorous results.

CREATIVE OPTIONS ▼

It Happens (15 to 20 minutes) Say: **One of the most painful things a teenager can face because of an imperfect family is the loss that comes with divorce, death, or separation. Please listen as I share an example.**

Chris was sixteen and his sister Kate was ten. Chris' parents had been married for eighteen years. For as long as Chris could remember, his parents never really argued, but they weren't really affectionate either. In fact, he noticed that they never really communicated at all.

Maybe that's why Chris wasn't surprised when he came home from practice to find his dad sitting in the family room staring blankly at an opened family album.

As he walked toward his dad, Chris heard his mom quietly direct, "Chris, get in the car—we're leaving."

"Where are we going?" asked Chris.

"To Aunt Kathy and Uncle Jim's."

In a frightened daze, Chris went outside and climbed into the front seat. His mom followed, dragging Kate along by the hand as Kate cried, "But I want to stay here with Daddy!"

It seemed that Kate instinctively knew the answer to the terrifying question Chris was about to ask: "What's going on, Mom?"

"Your dad and I are getting a divorce," she replied as she began to cry.

LEADER TIP for The Study

Because this topic can be so powerful and relevant to kids' lives, your group members may be tempted to get caught up in issues and lose sight of the deeper biblical principle found in The Point. Help your kids grasp The Point by guiding them to focus on the biblical investigation and by discussing how God's truth connects with reality in their lives.

Have kids form four groups. Give each group one of the four numbered situations in the "God Is With You" handout (p. 45). Give paper and pencils to Group 1 and 4. Give a sheet of newsprint and a marker to Group 3, and give paper and pencils to Group 2. Tell the groups they have five to ten minutes to prepare their responses to Chris' situation. Then ask each group to present its reaction. After all the groups have presented, call the students back together, and ask:

● **Do you think Chris will be a different person because of his parents' divorce? Why or why not?**

● **Do you think it would help Chris if you explained to him that <u>God is with us when we hurt?</u> Why or why not?**

Have students get into pairs. Ask all the kids to share with their partners a painful experience that they've encountered within their families. Direct kids to pray for each other's painful experiences. Encourage them to ask God to remind them that <u>he is with us when we hurt.</u> Have kids ask God to help them forgive their parents for times that they have failed to be perfect.

After the prayer, have kids share one way that they can tell that God is with their partners. For example, one student may say, "I can see how God has protected your sense of humor through the difficulties you have faced."

LEARNING PUZZLE ▼

Clip Art (10 to 15 minutes)
Give each student one of the paper clip puzzles you created before the study.

Say: **I have just given you another model of a family.** Ask:

● How could this model represent a family?

● How is the model unlike a family?

Then say: **Imagine that the paper clips with "Mom" and "Dad" taped to them stand for a mom and a dad in a family. Imagine that the two additional paper clips stand for their two children. As you look at the model, you'll notice that the mom and dad paper clips are connected to each other and both of the children clips are attached to each of the mom and the dad paper clips. Let's say that the connections between the paper clips symbolize the relationships between the members of the family. Your job is to disconnect the mom and the dad while making certain that neither of the children lose their connection with either of the parents at any time. Try to do that now.**

Let kids work on separating the mom and dad paper clips for a few minutes. Then have kids form groups of four, and ask:

● **How is what happened when you tried to disconnect the mom and the dad like what happens when a family breaks apart? How is it different?**

● **Is it possible for kids to stay connected to both of their parents if their parents have divorced or separated? Why or why not?**

● **Read Ephesians 6:1-3. How can we honor our parents when they're less than perfect?**

● **What are some ways we can honor our parents if they're divorced or separated?**

Say: **God loves those who get divorced and he loves their children also, but he hates the hurt and the strain that divorce causes for everyone involved. Fortunately, <u>God is there for you when you hurt.</u> It may seem difficult, but God wants you to have the best relationship possible with your parent or parents. He wants you to do the best you can to love and honor your parent or parents even though they aren't perfect. If you honor your parent or parents when they make mistakes, your love and respect will bring a little bit of healing to a broken home.**

LEADER TIP
for Clip Art

In order to give everyone a chance to solve the puzzle, have the students who finish first help those who are struggling. Don't worry if none of the kids are able to solve the puzzle. The activity will still be effective even if no one finds a solution.

DEPTH FINDER · I HATE DIVORCE

Malachi 2:13-16 makes it clear that God is against divorce. So why teach kids how to deal with the pain of divorce rather than equipping them with the skills to combat it? Part of the answer is found in role responsibility. It's not the children's responsibility to keep their parents together. A teenager shouldn't have to act as a diplomat, a counselor, or a best friend to his or her parents. That's not the teenager's role.

A child of divorced parents is responsible to honor both of his or her parents, to forgive his or her parents for their shortcomings, and to grieve the loss of previous family relationships. By understanding their role, kids may be spared the guilt and frustration that comes with trying to fill someone else's role.

How to Make a Paper Clip Puzzle

Create a "tag" on each of two paper clips by wrapping a piece of masking tape around the outer wire of each paper clip. Write "Mom" on one piece of tape, and write "Dad" on the other piece (see diagram "a"). Then add two more paper clips to create a puzzle that looks like the puzzle in diagram "b." Create the puzzle by looping the outer wire of the mom paper clip through the bottom arch of the dad paper clip. Thread the outer wire through the bottom arch until the paper clips are connected by their bottom arches. Leave the paper clips connected, and stack them one on top of the other. Thread the outer wire of an additional paper clip through the bottoms of both of the stacked (mom and dad) paper clips. Thread the outer wire of the fourth paper clip through both of the tops of the stacked (mom and dad) paper clips.

LEADER TIP

for Making Paper Clip Puzzles

If you don't have time to make a paper clip puzzle for each student, ask a volunteer to help you, or make one puzzle for every four students. Have kids work on the puzzles in groups of four during the "Clip Art" activity.

diagram "a"

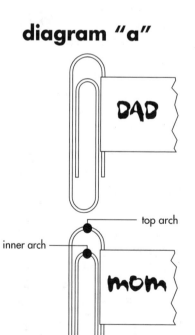

DAD

top arch

inner arch

mom

outer wire

bottom arch

diagram "b"

mom

THe SoLUtIoN to:

The Paper Clip Puzzle

Here is one way to solve the paper clip puzzle: Pull the two children paper clips to the bottom arches of the mom and dad paper clips (diagram "c1"). Pull the top arches of both the mom and dad paper clips away from each other (diagram "c2"). Loop the bottom arch of the mom paper clip around the inner arch of the dad paper clip while keeping both of the children paper clips at the bottom of the dad paper clip (diagram "c3"). Pull the bottom arch of the mom paper clip past the end of the inner wire on the dad paper clip.

diagram "c1"

diagram "c2"

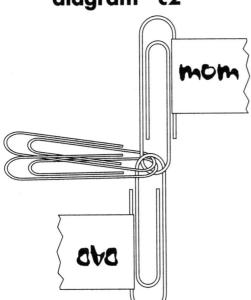

diagram "c3"

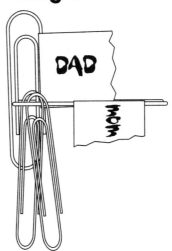

Ward and June

1. Your family goes to a local sporting event. While you're there, a man sitting in front of you passes gas in the youngest family member's face and spills beer on your entire family. During the game he shouts at the referee. At one point, he bumps into one of your family members and threatens to beat up your entire family. How does your family react?

● ●

2. Your family's car was totaled by a drunk driver. One of your family members died in the crash. The drunk driver was charged with vehicular homicide. Near the end of the drunk driver's trial, the judge asks each of the remaining family members if he or she would like to say anything to the driver. What does each person in your perfect family say?

● ●

3. Your family has decided to go out to eat. One family member wants to eat at "Chunks o' Lard." Another family member wants to eat at "Plates of Parsley." The rest of the family members don't have a preference. How does your family resolve the situation?

● ●

4. A next-door neighbor boy was disowned by his parents because he burned their house down. He served his sentence at the detention center. Now he's sixteen and has nowhere to go. Will your family let him live with you? How will you decide if he can stay at your house?

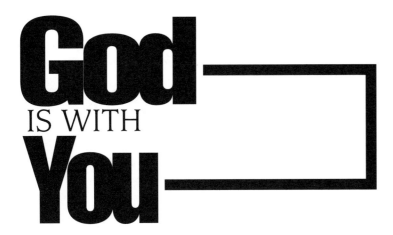

God
IS WITH
You

Group 1

Write two different endings to the story that show what Chris' life is like two years after the divorce. For the first ending, write the story as if Chris followed the advice in Psalms 40:1-3 and 120:1. Use Psalm 23 as a guide for your ending. Make certain you show how Chris' life would be different due to his response to the divorce.

For the second ending, write how Chris' life would turn out if he didn't follow the advice in Psalms 23; 40:1-3; and 120:1. Show the ways in which his life would be better (if any) and ways it would be worse if he didn't look to God for help through his parents' divorce.

● ●

Group 2

Present two role-plays of situations in which Chris asks you for advice. For the first response, imagine that Chris is a Christian friend of yours who wants to know the best way to deal with the hurt he feels. Decide how you would counsel Chris. Use Psalms 40:1-3 and 120:1 to show Chris what action he should take. Use Psalm 23 as source of encouragement.

For the second response, imagine that Chris isn't a Christian, but he still asks you for advice on how to handle the situation. Show how you would communicate the principles found in Psalms 23; 40:1-3; and 120:1. Show how your advice to Chris as a non-Christian would differ from the advice you'd give to Chris if he were a Christian.

● ●

Group 3

Make two columns on the sheet of newsprint you were given. In one column make a list of everything that would change in Chris' life because of his parents' divorce. Try to find comfort or advice in Psalms 23; 40:1-3; and 120:1 for how Chris should deal with each change you listed. Write your words of comfort and advice in the second column on the sheet of paper.

● ●

Group 4

Both of Chris' parents struggled with loneliness and depression after the divorce. Because of financial and relational pressures, Chris' parents seemed to care less about him than they did before. What could Chris say to his parents to make the transition smoother? Write a letter from Chris to his parents that explains his situation and struggles to them. In your letter, include encouragement and comfort for Chris' parents based on Psalms 23; 40:1-3; and 120:1.

Takin' Care of Busyness

Finding Peace in a Too-Busy World

by Debbie Gowensmith and Helen Turnbull

THE POINT:

God helps you deal with suffering.

■ Beep! Beep! Beep... ■ From the time their alarm clocks get them scrambling out of bed in the morning until their heads drop to their pillows at night, your young people are on the go, occupied with a variety of activities. Almost three-quarters of today's teenagers say they're involved in extracurricular activities (*America's Youth in the 1990s*); more than half say they work more than eleven hours a week; and almost half say they participate in church activities (Stephanie Martin, "The Too-Busy Myth About Kids," GROUP Magazine, May/June 1995). Add all that to their usual family and school obligations, and you can understand why many of your students seem to run at the speed of light. ■ But if you look past your students' busyness, you'll see a darker picture unfold. Today's teenagers report higher levels of stress, higher rates of suicide, and a higher amount of alcohol and drug abuse than previous generations of teenagers. ■ Why? ■ Perhaps the most appropriate question is "Why not?" Even if a young person makes it through adolescence without major tragedies, these years are still difficult. The happiest, most well-adjusted kids have problems with school, friends, and families. Every day brings new challenges and new changes. But many of today's kids face even more than these developmental issues. They've endured their parents' divorces; they've lived with the threat of violence at school and in their communities; they've been the targets of abuse—all in astounding numbers. Life feels unstable. No wonder they distract themselves with a flurry of activity. ■ But your kids can't afford to ignore their suffering. They need reassurance that someone is always there, ready to listen and comfort. This study encourages kids to take time from their busy lives to lean on the One who can best help them deal with their suffering.

The Study
AT A GLANCE

SECTION	MINUTES	WHAT STUDENTS WILL DO	SUPPLIES
Creative Opener	15 to 20	CHAOS ENCOUNTER—Try to finish tasks in a limited amount of time despite distractions.	Bibles, "Daily Planner Page" handouts (p. 56), "Chaos Cards" handouts (p. 56), pencils, scissors, adding machine tape, watch
Bible Exploration	15 to 20	T-MINUS 24 HOURS—Create time lines of what they'd do with their last twenty-four hours of life, then compare their time lines to a time line of how Jesus spent the twenty-four hours before his crucifixion.	Bibles, newsprint, tape, markers, pencils
Personal Reflection	10 to 15	CUP OF SUFFERING—Write down problems they face, then offer their problems to God.	Bibles, paper wads from the "Chaos Encounter" activity, pencils, large cups
Closing	5 to 10	PRAYER PLANNING—Set aside time to spend with God daily.	"Daily Planner Page" handouts from the "Chaos Encounter" activity, Bible, pencils

notes:

God helps you deal with suffering.

THE BIBLE CONNECTION

LUKE 10:38-42	Jesus teaches Mary and Martha the importance of putting work aside to spend time with him.
LUKE 22:39-46	Jesus turns to his Father during a time of tremendous suffering.
PHILIPPIANS 4:12-13	Paul describes the constant strength he finds in Jesus.

LEADER TIP
for The Study
Whenever groups discuss a list of questions, write the list on newsprint and tape it to a wall so groups can discuss the questions at their own pace.

In this study, kids will perform timed tasks amidst disruptions. Then they'll compare what they'd do with the last twenty-four hours of their lives to what Jesus did during the twenty-four hours before his crucifixion. Finally, kids will have the opportunity to take their own cup of suffering to God.

Through these experiences, kids can discover that when they slow down to spend time with God, he can help them through their pain.

Explore the verses in The Bible Connection, then examine the information in the Depthfinder boxes throughout the study to gain a deeper understanding of how these Scriptures connect with your young people.

BEFORE THE STUDY

For the "Chaos Encounter" activity, photocopy enough "Daily Planner Page" handouts (p. 56) for each person to have one. Also photocopy the "Chaos Cards" handout (p. 56), one for every four students, and cut out enough cards so each person can have one set of directions. Finally, cut adding machine tape into four-inch lengths. Make enough strips for each person in the class to have one, plus a few extras. If you don't have adding machine tape, cut two-by-four-inch strips from regular sheets of paper.

For the "T-Minus 24 Hours" activity, use the "Jesus' Last Day" Depthfinder to create on newsprint a time line of the last twenty-four hours before Jesus' crucifixion. Keep this time line hidden until the activity calls for it. Also tape several large sheets of newsprint to the walls of the room, and scatter assorted colors of markers below each sheet.

THE STUDY

CREATIVE OPENER ▼

LEADER TIP
for Chaos Encounter

It's OK if kids finish their tasks early or if they can't complete all of them. Whatever their status at the end of two minutes, your students will have sensed the chaotic mood, and the varied experiences will add to the discussion.

LEADER TIP
for Chaos Encounter

When you throw the paper wads, your kids' reactions will vary. Whether the entire group stops to acknowledge you, kids don't notice the wads, or kids respond in a variety of ways, don't discourage them. If you allow them to respond naturally, they'll have meaningful insights for the subsequent discussion.

Chaos Encounter (15 to 20 minutes)
When everyone has arrived, give each student a "Daily Planner Page" handout (p. 56) and a pencil. Say: **I've talked to many of you, and based on our conversations, I know that you guys lead really busy lives. Using your Daily Planner Page, write down what you do in a typical day from the time you wake up till the time you go to sleep.** After everyone has finished, have kids set aside their handouts for use later in the study.

Then say: **Now we're going to play a game. I'll give each of you a card containing a set of instructions. You'll have two minutes to fully complete all the tasks on your card.** Hand each person a set of instructions from the "Chaos Cards" handout (p. 56), then say: **I'll be keeping the official time on my watch. Ready? Go!**

As kids perform their tasks, create a chaotic mood by frequently calling out the time remaining. Also walk into the center of the room holding the strips of paper you prepared before the study. Make paper wads from the strips, and toss them randomly at kids' feet. Leave the wads where they fall, and allow kids to react to the wads however they wish.

After two minutes, call time. Then have kids form trios to discuss these questions:

● **What was your reaction to this game?**

DEPTHFINDER — PAUL'S SECRET OF HAPPINESS

The Apostle Paul faced more than his fair share of suffering. He was imprisoned many times for teaching others about Christ. He was beaten. He was denounced by fellow Jews, misunderstood by fellow Christians, and ostracized by Gentiles. He had more than enough reason to give in to fear and hatred. But Paul didn't wither or fade or fall into hatred. In fact, he lived with a deeply felt joy, and he communicated that joy in his letter to the Philippians. Despite the fact that Paul wrote this New Testament book while imprisoned in Rome, "The entire letter breathes Paul's radiant joy and serene happiness in Christ, even while in prison and in danger of death" *(The New Oxford Annotated Bible With the Apocrypha)*.

How did Paul keep such an admirable attitude under these dire circumstances? In Philippians 4:13, Paul revealed his secret: "I can do all things through Christ, because he gives me strength."

What a powerful example for all of us! Paul found joy despite burdensome circumstances because he took his suffering to God, and God gave him the strength he needed to endure it.

● **How was trying to finish all your tasks like living a busy life? How was it different?**

● **How were the wads of paper I threw at you like problems you face daily? How were they different?**

● **What was your response when I threw the paper wads? Why?**

● **How was that response like your response to personal problems that arise in your busy life? How was it different?**

After trios have finished discussing the questions, invite students to share their insights with the whole class. Then say: **Sometimes we fill our lives with so many activities and responsibilities that we end up pushing aside some of our most important issues. And just like those paper wads lying on the floor, our suffering doesn't disappear if we ignore it or are too busy to deal with it. Let's see what Jesus says about busyness.**

Tell students to return to their trios, and have one volunteer in each trio read aloud Luke 10:38-42. Then have trios discuss these questions:

● **Why do you think Mary and Martha reacted differently to Jesus' presence?**

● **What did Jesus say about that difference?**

● **Who are you more like: Mary or Martha? Why?**

● **Based on this Scripture, how do you think Mary would react to suffering in her life? What about Martha? Explain.**

● **From what you experienced in our game and from what Jesus said about Mary and Martha, what do you think would be a good response to suffering in your life? Explain.**

Say: **Putting aside busyness to face something painful can be really difficult. It forces us to feel the pain we'd much rather avoid. Fortunately, we don't have to face our suffering alone. <u>God helps us deal with suffering;</u> all we need to do is take the time to allow him to work in our lives.**

LEADER TIP for The Study

Because this topic can be so powerful and relevant to kids' lives, your group members may be tempted to get caught up in issues and lose sight of the deeper biblical principle found in The Point. Help your kids grasp The Point by guiding them to focus on the biblical investigation and by discussing how God's truth connects with reality in their lives.

BIBLE EXPLORATION ▼

T-Minus 24 Hours (15 to 20 minutes) Gather kids around you, and say: **Let's explore this idea a little deeper. Suppose you know you have only twenty-four hours left to live and that at the end of those twenty-four hours you'll be cruelly and painfully murdered. Think about all the things you'd want to accomplish in those last twenty-four hours—people you'd want to say goodbye to, places you'd want to go, things you'd want to do. Scatter around the room to the sheets of newsprint hanging on the walls, and find a space to write. Then create a time line of everything you'd want to achieve in your last twenty-four hours, beginning at 3 p.m. one day and ending at 3 p.m. the next. You have five minutes to complete your time line.**

While kids write, pick up the paper wads you dropped on the floor in the "Chaos Encounter" activity, and set them aside to use later. After five minutes, call time, and gather kids together. Bring out the time line of Jesus' last twenty-four hours (that you created before the study), and tape it to a wall in front of the kids.

Say: **This time line shows what Jesus did during his last twenty-four hours on earth. Jesus knew he had only twenty-four hours left; he knew he would be cruelly, painfully, unfairly murdered; and he knew who his murderers would be. With that background, let me show you how Jesus chose to spend those last, precious twenty-four hours.** Read the time line aloud, giving special emphasis to Jesus' time of prayer in the Garden of Gethsemane. Then have kids form groups of four to discuss these questions:

● **Compared to your predicted last day on earth, how busy was Jesus' last day?**

● **Why do you think Jesus chose to go to the Garden of Gethsemane to pray?**

● **Read Luke 22:39-46. According to this passage, how do you think Jesus felt about what was going to happen to him?**

● **How did he deal with those feelings?**

Say: **Jesus tried to accomplish a lot in the twenty-four hours before his crucifixion. But in the middle of that painful, difficult day, he set aside time to take his cup of suffering to God. He knew that to endure his crucifixion, he'd have to rely on his Father because <u>God helps us deal with suffering.</u>**

Have foursomes discuss these questions:

● **Why do you think Jesus confronted rather than avoided his suffering?**

● **Look at your time line. In your last twenty-four hours, would you have confronted your suffering? Why or why not?**

● **What might be the dangers of confronting suffering? What might be the benefits?**

● **What can you learn from Jesus' example?**

Say: **<u>God will help us deal with the suffering</u> we face in our lives if we allow him to. For that reason, no matter how busy we are, we must slow down long enough to take our cup of suffering to God.**

DEPTH FINDER UNDERSTANDING THE BIBLE

The story of Mary and Martha from Luke 10:38-42 demonstrates the importance of spending time with God. Mary's stirring act of devotion here—and Jesus' response to it—is strengthened further by the fact that Mary behaved in a way uncharacteristic for women of the day. With the arrival of important guests such as Jesus and his disciples, a woman would typically respond as Martha did, adopting the hostess role. Mary, however, took a place at Jesus' feet. This posture indicated discipleship—a male role—and would have "shocked most Jewish men." Jesus, however, welcomed Mary's attention. Although Martha's activity represented her devotion to Jesus, Mary's indicated even higher values. Jesus defended and complimented Mary's choice, encouraging her and Martha to seek God (Craig S. Keener, *The IVP Bible Background Commentary: New Testament*).

DEPTH FINDER   UNDERSTANDING THESE KIDS

Many of today's young people face some daunting problems. A Gallup Youth Survey poll shows that teenagers feel that the biggest problems facing their peers are drug abuse, alcohol abuse, peer pressure, AIDS, and teenage pregnancy. Yet when asked what problems they themselves face, their answers hit a little closer to home: school grades, career uncertainties, growing pains, fears, and getting along with parents (*America's Youth in the 1990s*).

If you look at the results of this survey, you might be tempted to apply those results to most of your young people and dismiss their potential for experiencing pain. You might think you need to concentrate more attention on those students who face the daunting problems, leaving the students with more "mundane" struggles to cope alone. If you find yourself jumping to these conclusions, think again. In a study about adolescent stress, researcher Inge Seiffge-Krenke found that "in the ordinary transactions in the lives of adolescents, it was not so much a major event, but a continuous series of irritating, frustrating, and distressing events that mattered most." Kids in Seiffge-Krenke's study cited stressful events such as getting bad grades, arguing with teachers or with parents, and struggling with friendships—things that happen every day (*Stress, Coping, and Relationships in Adolescence*). These common events cause many of your young people pain and consternation that they probably mask by overinvolving themselves in activities.

So don't be fooled by kids who haven't experienced tragedy or major upheaval. They aren't immune to suffering. No matter what life has dealt them, *all* of your students need to know that God will help them through their suffering.

PERSONAL REFLECTION ▼

Cup of Suffering

(10 to 15 minutes)
Hand each person a pencil and a paper wad from the "Chaos Encounters" activity. Ask kids to scatter throughout the room so that each person can be alone. After kids have settled into their own spaces, say: **We all face personal suffering, and when we stop to think, we often discover problems we've been avoiding. As difficult as this is, let's give it a try right now. Flatten out your paper wad, and write on it something you worry about or a problem you face. Then fold up your paper.** Give kids a couple of minutes to think and write, and fill out a paper wad yourself. Then gather kids together to form a circle and sit down. Hold up the large cup, and say: **Though facing our suffering is difficult, we don't have to endure it alone. <u>God helps us deal with suffering</u> when we allow him to.**

We're going to pass this cup around the circle. When the cup comes to you, you have the choice of putting your paper in the cup as a symbol of handing your problem to God. If you choose to put your paper in the cup, say the following as you do so: "Lord, please take this cup of suffering." Start with yourself, then pass the cup to a person sitting next to you. When the cup returns to

LEADER TIP
for Cup of Suffering
To ensure that you'll have enough room in the cup for every paper, make sure kids fold their papers instead of crumpling them into wads again. If you have a large class and need a larger container, substitute a paper bag or a large pitcher.

you, have the kids form pairs to discuss these questions:

● **How did you feel when you had the choice of handing your problem to God?**

● **How will this experience affect what you do with personal suffering on a daily basis?**

Then have each person pray for his or her partner, asking for God's help in making time to deal with suffering. After a minute, finish the prayer for the whole group by praying aloud: **Dear God, thank you for helping us deal with our suffering. Help us to remember to make time in our busy lives to bring our cup of suffering to you. Amen.**

CLOSING ▼

Prayer Planning (5 to 10 minutes)

Have kids retrieve their "Daily Planner Page" handouts from the first activity, and hand out pencils. Say: **Paul, a great disciple, was imprisoned many times for teaching others about Jesus. I'm going to read an excerpt of a letter he wrote from prison to a congregation of Christians.** Read aloud Philippians 4:12-13. Say: **Paul suffered for his faith and for telling others about Jesus. But through his faith in Jesus, he found the strength he needed to continue with high spirits. God helped Paul deal with his suffering, and God will help you deal with suffering, too. All you have to do is make the time to bring your problems to him.**

Look at your daily planner page. If you didn't include some time to spend with God in your typical day, you may choose to pencil time in now. Pause for kids to do this if they want. **Now, on the top of your sheet in the "Don't Forget:" space, write Philippians 4:13: "I can do all things through Christ, because he gives me strength."** Encourage kids to take their daily planner pages home and place them where their pages can remind them to spend time with God every day.

DEPTHFINDER JESUS' LAST DAY

No person knew more about dealing with suffering under pressure than Jesus. In his final hours, Jesus had to prepare his disciples for his death, and he had to warn them of the suffering they'd face after he was gone. In the midst of this frenzy and with the knowledge of a looming, horrible death, Jesus knew he had to spend time with his Father, and he did so at Gethsemane.

This time line will help your kids realize how they can always take time to bring their suffering—regardless of the gravity of their problems—to God.

Thursday

3 p.m.–10 p.m.
Jesus prepares for the Passover meal (Luke 22:7-13).
Jesus shares the Last Supper with his disciples (Luke 22:14-22).
Jesus washes his disciples' feet (John 13:1-17).

10 p.m.–12 a.m.
Jesus prays in the Garden of Gethsemane (Luke 22:39-46).
Judas betrays Jesus (Luke 22:47-48).
Jesus heals the priest's servant (Luke 22:49-51).
Jesus is arrested (Luke 22:52-54a).

Friday

12:30 a.m.–2:30 a.m.
Three times Peter denies knowing Jesus (Luke 22:55-62).
Jesus faces mocking by the soldiers who guard him at a high priest's house (Luke 22:63-65).

sunrise
Jesus is put on trial by elders (Luke 22:66-71).

morning
Jesus goes before Pilate (Luke 23:1-5).
Jesus goes before Herod (Luke 23:6-11a).
Jesus goes before Pilate a second time, is rejected by the crowd, and is sentenced to death (Luke 23:11b-25).

12 p.m.–3 p.m.
Jesus walks to The Skull, teaching along the way (Luke 23:26-31).
Jesus is crucified (Luke 23:33).
Jesus asks God to forgive his enemies (Luke 23:34).
Jesus dies on the cross (Luke 23:44-46).

(Source: Craig S. Keener, *The IVP Bible Background Commentary: New Testament*)

Daily Planner Page

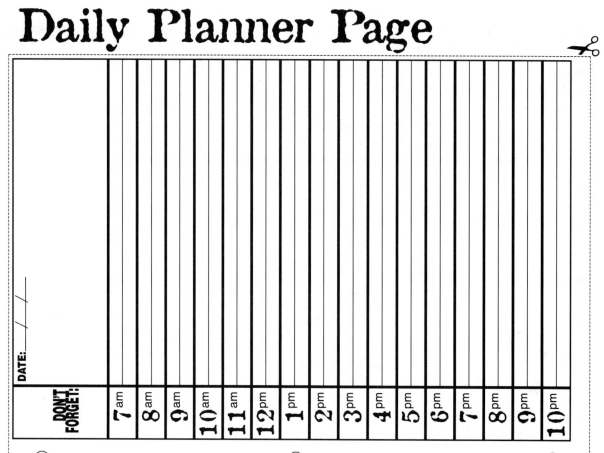

DATE: ___/___/___

DON'T FORGET:

7am | 8am | 9am | 10am | 11am | 12pm | 1pm | 2pm | 3pm | 4pm | 5pm | 6pm | 7pm | 8pm | 9pm | 10pm

Chaos Cards

CARD

1
1. Find two people wearing red, and pay each a compliment.
2. Tell someone you don't know very well what your favorite holiday is and why.
3. Walk around the room backward twice while humming the national anthem.
4. Read Luke 10:38-42.

2
1. Find two people wearing blue, and pay each a compliment.
2. Sing your favorite Christmas carol to a member of the opposite sex.
3. "Skate" a figure eight while balancing a Bible on your head.
4. Read Luke 10:38-42.

3
1. Find two people wearing white, and pay each a compliment.
2. Tell someone with glasses what your favorite TV show is and why.
3. Pantomime a scene from The Wizard of Oz.
4. Read Luke 10:38-42.

4
1. Find two people wearing black, and pay each a compliment.
2. Sing "Happy Birthday" in an Elmer Fudd voice to someone with brown hair.
3. Do jumping jacks from one end of the room to the other end.
4. Read Luke 10:38-42.

why ▼ Active and Interactive Learning works with teenagers

Let's Start With the Big Picture

Think back to a major life lesson you've learned.
Got it? Now answer these questions:
● Did you learn your lesson from something you read?
● Did you learn it from something you heard?
● Did you learn it from something you experienced?

If you're like 99 percent of your peers, you answered "yes" only to the third question—you learned your life lesson from something you experienced.

This simple test illustrates the most convincing reason for using active and interactive learning with young people: People learn best through experience. Or to put it even more simply, people learn by doing.

Learning by doing is what active learning is all about. No more sitting quietly in chairs and listening to a speaker expound theories about God—that's passive learning. Active learning gets kids out of their chairs and into the experience of life. With active learning, kids get to *do* what they're studying. They *feel* the effects of the principles you teach. They *learn* by experiencing truth firsthand.

Active learning works because it recognizes three basic learning needs and uses them in concert to enable young people to make discoveries on their own and to find practical life applications for the truths they believe.

So what are these three basic learning needs?
1. Teenagers need action.
2. Teenagers need to think.
3. Teenagers need to talk.

Read on to find out exactly how these needs will be met by using the active and interactive learning techniques in Group's Core Belief Bible Study Series in your youth group.

1. Teenagers Need Action

Aircraft pilots know well the difference between passive and active learning. Their passive learning comes through listening to flight instructors and reading flight-instruction books. Their active learning comes through actually flying an airplane or flight simulator. Books and lectures may be helpful, but pilots really learn to fly by manipulating a plane's controls themselves.

We can help young people learn in a similar way. Though we may engage students passively in some reading and listening to teachers, their understanding and application of God's Word will really take off through simulated and real-life experiences.

Forms of active learning include simulation games; role-plays; service projects; experiments; research projects; group pantomimes; mock trials; construction projects; purposeful games; field trips; and, of course, the most powerful form of active learning—real-life experiences.

We can more fully explain active learning by exploring four of its characteristics:

● **Active learning is an adventure.** Passive learning is almost always predictable. Students sit passively while the teacher or speaker follows a planned outline or script.

In active learning, kids may learn lessons the teacher never envisioned. Because the leader trusts students to help create the learning experience, learners may venture into unforeseen discoveries. And often the teacher learns as much as the students.

● **Active learning is fun and captivating.** What are we communicating when we say, "OK, the fun's over—time to talk about God"? What's the hidden message? That joy is separate from God? And that learning is separate from joy?

What a shame.

Active learning is not joyless. One seventh-grader we interviewed clearly remembered her best Sunday school lesson: "Jesus was the light, and we went into a dark room and shut off the lights. We had a candle, and we learned that Jesus is the light and the dark can't shut off the light." That's active learning. Deena enjoyed the lesson. She had fun. And she learned.

Active learning intrigues people. Whether they find a foot-washing experience captivating or maybe a bit uncomfortable, they learn. And they learn on a level deeper than any work sheet or teacher's lecture could ever reach.

● **Active learning involves everyone.** Here the difference between passive and active learning becomes abundantly clear. It's like the difference between watching a football game on television and actually playing in the game.

The "trust walk" provides a good example of involving everyone in active learning. Half of the group members put on blindfolds; the other half serve as guides. The "blind" people trust the guides to lead them through the building or outdoors. The guides prevent the blind people from falling down stairs or tripping over rocks. Everyone needs to participate to learn the inherent lessons of trust, faith, doubt, fear, confidence, and servanthood. Passive spectators of this experience would learn little, but participants learn a great deal.

● **Active learning is focused through debriefing.** Activity simply for activity's sake doesn't usually result in good learning. Debriefing— evaluating an experience by discussing it in pairs or small groups— helps focus the experience and draw out its meaning. Debriefing helps sort and order the information students gather during the experience. It helps learners relate the recently experienced activity to their lives.

The process of debriefing is best started immediately after an experience. We use a three-step process in debriefing: reflection, interpretation, and application.

Reflection—This first step asks the students, "How did you feel?" Active-learning experiences typically evoke an emotional reaction, so it's appropriate to begin debriefing at that level.

Some people ask, "What do feelings have to do with education?" Feelings have everything to do with education. Think back again to that time in your life when you learned a big lesson. In all likelihood, strong feelings accompanied that lesson. Our emotions tend to cement things into our memories.

When you're debriefing, use open-ended questions to probe feelings. Avoid questions that can be answered with a "yes" or "no." Let your learners know that there are no wrong answers to these "feeling" questions. Everyone's feelings are valid.

Interpretation—The next step in the debriefing process asks, "What does this mean to you? How is this experience like or unlike some other aspect of your life?" Now you're asking people to identify a message or principle from the experience.

You want your learners to discover the message for themselves. So instead of telling students your answers, take the time to ask questions that encourage self-discovery. Use Scripture and discussion in pairs or small groups to explore how the actions and effects of the activity might translate to their lives.

Alert! Some of your people may interpret wonderful messages that you never intended. That's not failure! That's the Holy Spirit at work. God allows us to catch different glimpses of his kingdom even when we all look through the same glass.

Application—The final debriefing step asks, "What will you do about it?" This step moves learning into action. Your young people have shared a common experience. They've discovered a principle. Now they must create something new with what they've just experienced and interpreted. They must integrate the message into their lives.

The application stage of debriefing calls for a decision. Ask your students how they'll change, how they'll grow, what they'll do as a result of your time together.

2. Teenagers Need to Think

Today's students have been trained not to think. They aren't dumber than previous generations. We've simply conditioned them not to use their heads.

You see, we've trained our kids to respond with the simplistic answers they think the teacher wants to hear. Fill-in-the-blank student workbooks and teachers who ask dead-end questions such as "What's the capital of Delaware?" have produced kids and adults who have learned not to think.

And it doesn't just happen in junior high or high school. Our children are schooled very early not to think. Teachers attempt to help kids read with nonsensical fill-in-the-blank drills, word scrambles, and missing-letter puzzles.

Helping teenagers think requires a paradigm shift in how we teach. We need to plan for and set aside time for higher-order thinking and be willing to reduce our time spent on lower-order parroting. Group's Core Belief Bible Study Series is designed to help you do just that.

Thinking classrooms look quite different from traditional classrooms. In most church environments, the teacher does most of the talking and hopes that knowledge will transmit from his or her brain to the students'. In thinking settings, the teacher coaches students to ponder, wonder, imagine, and problem-solve.

3. Teenagers Need to Talk

Everyone knows that the person who learns the most in any class is the teacher. Explaining a concept to someone else is usually more helpful to the explainer than to the listener. So why not let the students do more teaching? That's one of the chief benefits of letting kids do the talking. This process is called interactive learning.

What is interactive learning? Interactive learning occurs when students discuss and work cooperatively in pairs or small groups.

Interactive learning encourages learners to work together. It honors the fact that students can learn from one another, not just from the teacher. Students work together in pairs or small groups to accomplish shared goals. They build together, discuss together, and present together. They teach each other and learn from one another. Success as a group is celebrated. Positive interdependence promotes individual and group learning.

Interactive learning not only helps people learn but also helps learners feel better about themselves and get along better with others. It accomplishes these things more effectively than the independent or competitive methods.

Here's a selection of interactive learning techniques that are used in Group's Core Belief Bible Study Series. With any of these models, leaders may assign students to specific partners or small groups. This will maximize cooperation and learning by preventing all the "rowdies" from linking up. And it will allow for new friendships to form outside of established cliques.

Following any period of partner or small-group work, the leader may reconvene the entire class for large-group processing. During this time the teacher may ask for reports or discoveries from individuals or teams. This technique builds in accountability for the teacherless pairs and small groups.

Pair-Share—With this technique each student turns to a partner and responds to a question or problem from the teacher or leader. Every learner responds. There are no passive observers. The teacher may then ask people to share their partners' responses.

Study Partners—Most curricula and most teachers call for Scripture passages to be read to the whole class by one person. One reads; the others doze.

Why not relinquish some teacher control and let partners read and react with each other? They'll all be involved—and will learn more.

Learning Groups—Students work together in small groups to create a model, design artwork, or study a passage or story; then they discuss what they learned through the experience. Each person in the learning group may be assigned a specific role. Here are some examples:

Reader

Recorder (makes notes of key thoughts expressed during the reading or discussion)

Checker (makes sure everyone understands and agrees with answers arrived at by the group)

Encourager (urges silent members to share their thoughts)

When everyone has a specific responsibility, knows what it is, and contributes to a small group, much is accomplished and much is learned.

Summary Partners—One student reads a paragraph, then the partner summarizes the paragraph or interprets its meaning. Partners alternate roles with each paragraph.

The paraphrasing technique also works well in discussions. Anyone who wishes to share a thought must first paraphrase what the previous person said. This sharpens listening skills and demonstrates the power of feedback communication.

Jigsaw—Each person in a small group examines a different concept, Scripture, or part of an issue. Then each teaches the others in the group. Thus, all members teach, and all must learn the others' discoveries. This technique is called a jigsaw because individuals are responsible to their group for different pieces of the puzzle.

JIGSAW EXAMPLE

Here's an example of a jigsaw.

Assign four-person teams. Have teammates each number off from one to four. Have all the Ones go to one corner of the room, all the Twos to another corner, and so on.

Tell team members they're responsible for learning information in their numbered corners and then for teaching their team members when they return to their original teams.

Give the following assignments to various groups:

Ones: Read Psalm 22. Discuss and list the prophecies made about Jesus.

Twos: Read Isaiah 52:13–53:12. Discuss and list the prophecies made

about Jesus.

Threes: Read Matthew 27:1-32. Discuss and list the things that happened to Jesus.

Fours: Read Matthew 27:33-66. Discuss and list the things that happened to Jesus.

After the corner groups meet and discuss, instruct all learners to return to their original teams and report what they've learned. Then have each team determine which prophecies about Jesus were fulfilled in the passages from Matthew.

Call on various individuals in each team to report one or two prophecies that were fulfilled.

You Can Do It Too!

All this information may sound revolutionary to you, but it's really not. God has been using active and interactive learning to teach his people for generations. Just look at Abraham and Isaac, Jacob and Esau, Moses and the Israelites, Ruth and Boaz. And then there's Jesus, who used active learning all the time!

Group's Core Belief Bible Study Series makes it easy for you to use active and interactive learning with your group. The active and interactive elements are automatically built in! Just follow the outlines, and watch as your kids grow through experience and positive interaction with others.

FOR DEEPER STUDY

For more information on incorporating active and interactive learning into your work with teenagers, check out these resources:

● *Why Nobody Learns Much of Anything at Church: And How to Fix It,* by Thom and Joani Schultz (Group Publishing) and
● *Do It! Active Learning in Youth Ministry,* by Thom and Joani Schultz (Group Publishing).

your evaluation of

Bible Study Series
for senior high

why SUFFERING matters

Group Publishing, Inc.
Attention: Core Belief Talk-back
P.O. Box 481
Loveland, CO 80539
Fax: (970) 669-1994

Please help us continue to provide innovative and useful resources for ministry. After you've led the studies in this volume, take a moment to fill out this evaluation; then mail or fax it to us at the address above. Thanks!

● ● ● ● ● ●

1. As a whole, this book has been (circle one)

not very helpful   very helpful

1   2   3   4   5   6   7   8   9   10

2. The best things about this book:

3. How this book could be improved:

4. What I will change because of this book:

5. Would you be interested in field-testing future Core Belief Bible Studies and giving us your feedback? If so, please complete the information below:

Name _____

Street address _____

City _____ State _____ Zip _____

Daytime telephone (____) _____ Date _____

THANKS!